WHATEVER HAPPENED?

THE ANCIENT ROMANS

BY KIRSTY HOLMES

Enslow
PUBLISHING

Published in 2021 by Enslow Publishing, LLC
101 W. 23rd Street, Suite 240,
New York, NY 10011

Copyright © 2021 Booklife Publishing
This edition is published by arrangement with
Booklife Publishing.

All rights reserved.

No part of this book may be reproduced by any
means without the written permission of the
publisher.

Cataloging-in-Publication Data

Names: Holmes, Kirsty.
Title: The ancient Romans / Kirsty Holmes.
Description: New York : Enslow Publishing, 2021. |
Series: Whatever happened? | Includes glossary
and index.
Identifiers: ISBN 9781978519831 (pbk.) | ISBN
9781978519855 (library bound) | ISBN 9781978519848
(6 pack)
Subjects: LCSH: Rome--History--Juvenile literature. |
Rome--Civilization--Juvenile literature.
Classification: LCC DG77.H65 2020 | DDC 937--dc23

Printed in the United States of America

CPSIA compliance information: Batch #BS20ENS: For further
information contact Enslow Publishing, New York, New York at
1-800-542-2595

BC AND AD

In this book, you will see **BC** after and **AD** before some dates. And some of the dates might look backwards. What's going on?

AD stands for Anno Domini and that means "in the year of the Lord". Christian calendars count forwards from the year they believe Jesus Christ was born. When you see AD, you are counting forwards on the timeline.
AD 1750 = 1,750 years after Jesus was born.

BC stands for Before Christ. If you see this next to a date, it means this happened before the birth of Jesus Christ. When you see BC, you are counting backwards on the timeline.
1750 BC = 1,750 years before Jesus was born.

When describing a range of dates, you always count forwards.
So "between 1500 and 500 BC" or "from AD 500 to AD 1500" is correct.

Check back here if you need to.

2000 BC **1500 BC** **1000 BC** **500 BC** JESUS

WRITE THE YEAR AND THEN BC

CONTENTS

PAGE 4	WHATEVER HAPPENED TO THE ANCIENT ROMANS?
PAGE 6	WHO WERE THE ANCIENT ROMANS?
PAGE 8	PAX ROMANA
PAGE 10	EMPERORS BEHAVING BADLY
PAGE 12	THE FIVE GOOD EMPERORS
PAGE 14	CIVIL WAR
PAGE 16	THE CRISIS OF THE THIRD CENTURY
PAGE 18	EAST MEETS WEST
PAGE 20	CONSTANTINE
PAGE 22	THE GOTHS
PAGE 24	THE END OF THE WEST
PAGE 26	OH NO! ODOACER!
PAGE 28	WHAT REMAINS OF THE ANCIENTS?
PAGE 30	GLOSSARY
PAGE 32	INDEX

WORDS THAT LOOK LIKE THIS ARE EXPLAINED IN THE GLOSSARY ON PAGES 30 AND 31.

BORN — AD 500 — AD 1000 — AD 1500 — AD 2000

WRITE AD AND THEN THE YEAR

WHATEVER HAPPENED TO THE ANCIENT ROMANS?

GLADIATORS, ET CETERA...

Imagine ancient Rome. I bet you're imagining bronzed gladiators training in the arena. Maybe you're thinking of rows of **LEGIONARIES**, with armor gleaming in the sunlight? Or perhaps you are thinking of Mars, god of war, or Jupiter, ruler of the skies? Yep – you certainly know who the ancient Romans were! Clever you. But have you ever wondered where they went?

Where did the **CULTURE**, people, and traditions of one of the world's most **ICONIC** civilizations go?

IN ANCIENT POMPEII, PART OF THE ANCIENT ROMAN WORLD, PEOPLE WROTE ON THE WALLS THEIR THOUGHTS ABOUT LIFE. THIS IS GRAFFITI.

TODAY, IN VERONA, ITALY, PEOPLE WRITE MESSAGES OF LOVE ON THE WALLS.

OH NO! SOMEONE'S DRAWN ALL OVER THIS OLD BIT OF WALL! DON'T WORRY. I'LL HAVE THAT CLEAN IN NO TIME!!

STOP! THAT'S PRICELESS ROMAN GRAFFITI!

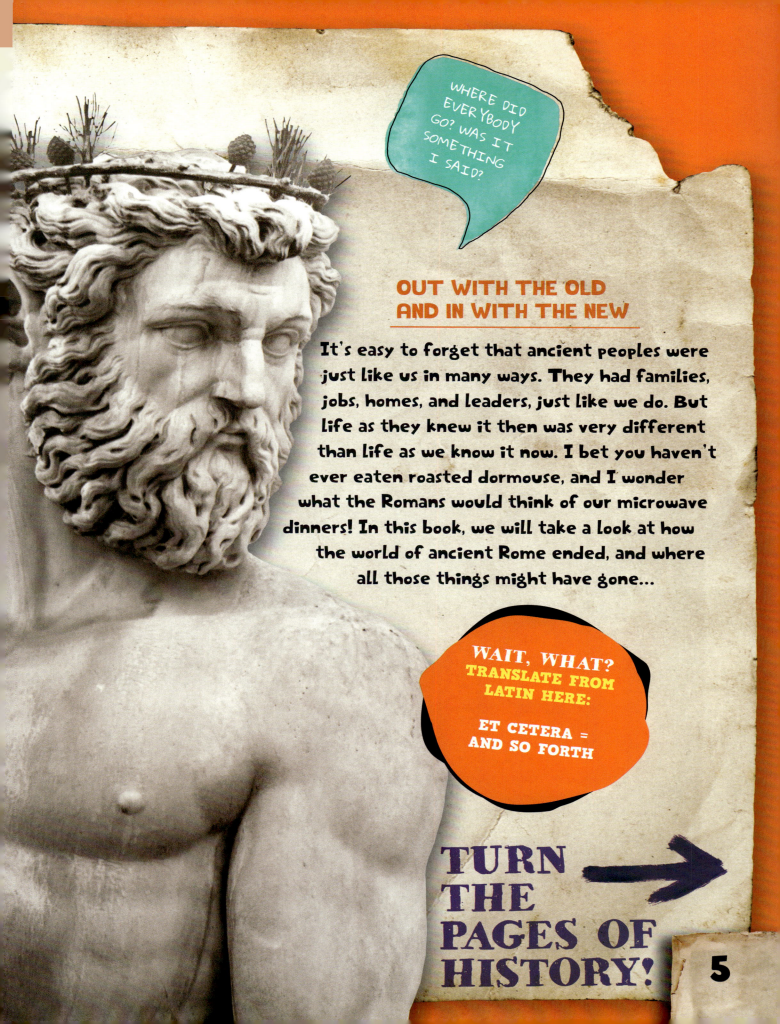

WHERE DID EVERYBODY GO? WAS IT SOMETHING I SAID?

OUT WITH THE OLD AND IN WITH THE NEW

It's easy to forget that ancient peoples were just like us in many ways. They had families, jobs, homes, and leaders, just like we do. But life as they knew it then was very different than life as we know it now. I bet you haven't ever eaten roasted dormouse, and I wonder what the Romans would think of our microwave dinners! In this book, we will take a look at how the world of ancient Rome ended, and where all those things might have gone...

WAIT, WHAT?
TRANSLATE FROM LATIN HERE:

ET CETERA = AND SO FORTH

TURN THE PAGES OF HISTORY! →

WHO WERE THE ANCIENT ROMANS?

WHERE ON EARTH?

The Roman Empire was, well, MASSIVE....

FAMOUS FOR:
- Gladiators
- Legionaries
- Generals

Rome

Why do legionaries always have sore feet? Because they're always Roman around!

I just hope you are better at fighting than telling jokes...

LEGIONARIES

GENERALS

GLADIATORS

OK, men. That was a great day of training. Who's up for a bath?

ROMAN BATHS WERE USED FOR BATHING AND MEETING OTHER ROMANS. THESE BATHS ARE IN A TOWN CALLED BATH IN THE UK.

OH, GODS!

The Romans believed in lots of gods who were each in charge of different things. For example, Jupiter was the leader of the Roman gods. He had control of the sky and lightning.

THUNDERBOLTS AND LIGHTNING. VERY, VERY FRIGHTENING...

THE FAMILIA

The oldest male in a family was in charge. He was known as the paterfamilias. The paterfamilias was usually the only person who could own property or make decisions. The paterfamilias decided who got to join a familia through **ADOPTION**. Everyone else in the familia belonged to the paterfamilias as if they were property, and he got to decide everything about their lives – including being able to put them to death if he wished.

Paterfamilias — The head of the familia

Materfamilias — The wife of the paterfamilias

Sons — By birth or adoption, sons can start their own families by marriage or stay in the familia

Daughters — The paterfamilias usually decides who daughters marry. They leave upon marriage to join their new husband's family.

DAUGHTERS-IN-LAW — Upon marriage they become part of the familia

Grandchildren — May be part of their father's family or remain under control of the paterfamilias

Freedmen — Freed slaves who were loyal to the familia but were free to start their own familia

Skilled slaves — Skilled or educated slaves could hope to become freed

Unskilled slaves — Had no power

WAIT, WHAT? TO PRONOUNCE THIS WORD, SAY: PATERFAMILIAS = PAY-TER-FAM-ILLY-AS

PAX ROMANA

TIME TO CHILL OUT

From the **REIGN** of Augustus (27 BC to AD 14) to the end of the time of Marcus Aurelius (AD 161 to AD 180), the Roman world was, more or less, at peace. This was called the Pax Romana – "pax" means peace in Latin. The Roman Empire protected each **PROVINCE** and the provinces were allowed to make their own laws, as long as they accepted being controlled by Rome.

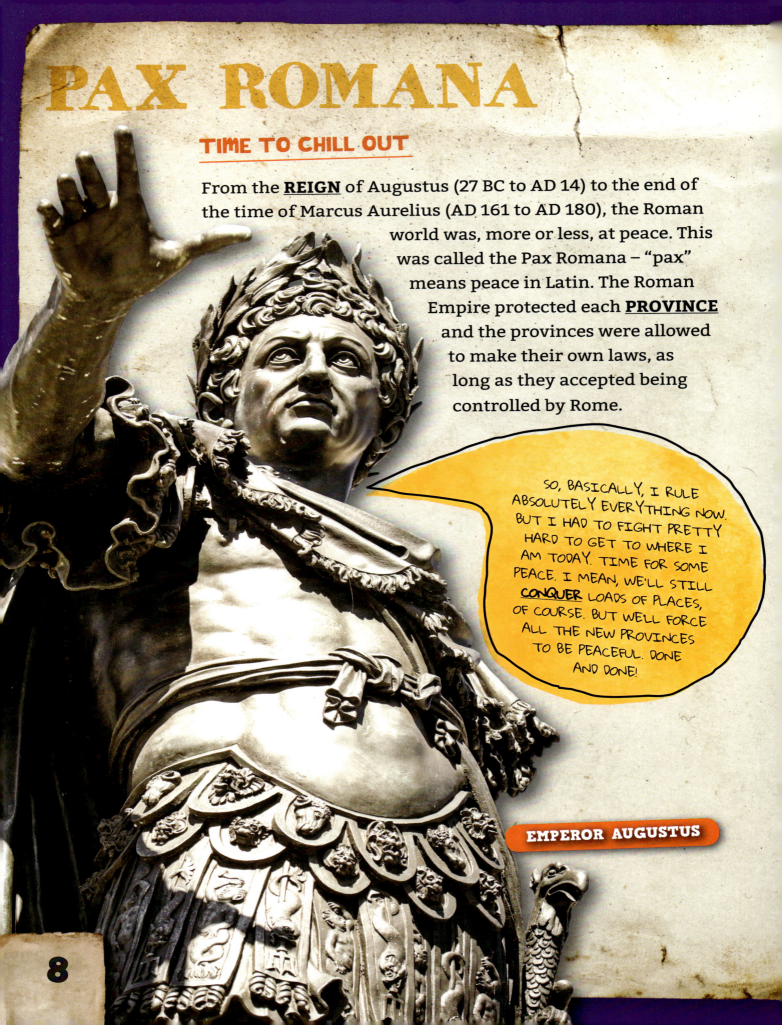

SO, BASICALLY, I RULE ABSOLUTELY EVERYTHING NOW. BUT I HAD TO FIGHT PRETTY HARD TO GET TO WHERE I AM TODAY. TIME FOR SOME PEACE. I MEAN, WE'LL STILL **CONQUER** LOADS OF PLACES, OF COURSE. BUT WE'LL FORCE ALL THE NEW PROVINCES TO BE PEACEFUL. DONE AND DONE!

EMPEROR AUGUSTUS

THESE ARE GOOD TIMES TO BE A FARMER IN ANCIENT ROME.

I FOUND ROME A CITY OF BRICK, AND LEFT IT ONE OF MARBLE. PAT ON THE BACK FOR ME... NOW COULD SOMEONE GET THIS BABY OFF MY LEG, PLEASE?

GOLD STAR FOR AUGUSTUS

Augustus did a great job of running Rome itself. He made sure everyone would be okay if there was a fire or a flood, and made sure there wouldn't be FAMINES for the people of Rome. He took charge of the water, roads, and food; made the police force bigger; and rebuilt temples. The next few emperors kept the peace going. Pax Romana would last almost 200 years.

WAIT, WHAT?
TO PRONOUNCE THESE WORDS, SAY:

AUGUSTUS = UH-GUS-TUSS

MARCUS AURELIUS = MAR-CUSS OR-AY-LEE-US

EMPERORS BEHAVING BADLY

THE TROUBLE WITH EMPERORS

The emperors of Rome could be good, and they could be bad. The trouble with emperors was that they had absolute power — this meant they could do whatever they wanted. This sounds great, but the type of person who might have wanted that kind of power might not have been the kind of person you would have wanted to be emperor...

I'M EMPEROR CALIGULA. PEOPLE MIGHT HAVE THOUGHT IT WAS A GOOD IDEA WHEN I BECAME EMPEROR, BUT I SOON SHOWED THEM! HA HA HA HA! I'M ABSOLUTELY CRAZY! NOW I'VE DECIDED I AM A GOD! ALSO, MY HORSE IS A CONSUL NOW! WOO-HOO!

> YO! I'M NERO! MY MOM, AGRIPPINA, WAS HORRIBLE AND CONTROLLING... SO OBVIOUSLY I HAD HER MURDERED. HA HA! NOW I CAN GET ON WITH BEING THE ROCK STAR THAT I CLEARLY AM. YOU SHOULD HEAR ME ON THE **LYRE**. WHAT'S THAT? ROME IS ON FIRE? WHAT, ALL OF IT? OH DEAR... I'VE BEEN TOO BUSY LEARNING ALL THESE INSTRUMENTS TO KNOW WHAT TO DO! OOPS!

> MY NAME IS DOMITIAN. I'M NOT LIKE A NORMAL EMPEROR— I'M A FUN EMPEROR. I LIKE SPORTS AND GAMES AND FUN AND I ESPECIALLY LIKE CHARIOTS! BUT... I'M PRETTY SURE EVERYONE IS TRYING TO KILL ME. I MEAN, WHY WOULDN'T THEY? MAYBE EVEN MY WIFE IS TRYING TO KILL ME. AARGH! THEY'RE ALL OUT TO GET ME! SEND OUT THE SPIES!

Did these party animals cause the end of the Roman Empire? We're going to look at the story of the slow fall of one of humanity's greatest-ever civilizations. It's a great story. And at the end, you can make up your own mind, young historian: whatever happened to the ancient Romans?

WAIT, WHAT?
TO PRONOUNCE THESE WORDS, SAY:

CALIGULA = CAL-IG-YOO-LA
NERO = NEAR-OH
DOMITIAN = DOM-ISH-UN

THE FIVE GOOD EMPERORS

AD 96 to AD 180

The high point of the Roman Empire was when it was ruled over by five emperors who were very different from the party-loving, strange emperors before them. These emperors were not related by birth. Instead, each emperor chose someone who would be the next emperor, and then adopted him. The first of this line was Nerva, a **POLITICIAN**, who took over after Domitian was **ASSASSINATED**.

DOMITIAN WAS KILLED BY MURDERERS IN AD 96.

Nerva adopted Trajan, who became emperor in AD 98. Trajan had been ruling in Upper Germany, and was a great general. He treated the senate with respect, looked after the people, and may even have given money to poor children in the Italian cities.

EMPEROR TRAJAN

12

"I LOVE EMPEROR TRAJAN! NOW I GET HELP FROM THE GOVERNMENT. MY MAMA GETS FREE GRAIN NOW, AND WE DON'T HAVE TO BE HUNGRY ANYMORE. I WANT TO JOIN THE ARMY WHEN I GROW UP!"

Trajan adopted his cousin, Hadrian, who became emperor when Trajan died. Hadrian was a great builder, and strong walls were put up in England and Germany. He made the empire even bigger and brought the Roman people together. Hadrian passed the emperor title to Antonius Pius, and also demanded that Pius must pass it to Marcus Aurelius, which he did. Each man chose another with proven skills or talents, and each of these emperors brought something good to the empire. For many, many years, Rome was at its most glorious...

THIS IS WHAT IS LEFT OF HADRIAN'S WALL, BUILT BETWEEN ENGLAND AND SCOTLAND.

"AH, WHERE DID EVERYTHING GO WRONG?"

"NO IDEA, SIR. CAKE?"

... so what on Earth happened?

CIVIL WAR

GO ON, MY SON

Some say the beginning of the end started with Marcus Aurelius's son, Commodus. Marcus Aurelius did something different than the other "Five Good Emperors" – he named his own son as **HEIR**.

> HEY! I'M THE EMPEROR NOW! WOO-HOO! I DON'T KNOW WHY EVERYONE IS SAYING I'M TOO RICH AND NOT SERIOUS ENOUGH. WHAT? THIS? THIS IS MY LION HAT. IT'S MADE FROM A REAL LION, SO YOU KNOW IT'S GOOD.

Commodus was more like Caligula and Nero—he liked to live a rich life. He was assassinated by his own ministers and Rome broke out into **CIVIL WAR**. Rome then had five emperors in just one year.

COMMODUS

"WHO'S EMPEROR NOW, THEN?"

"PERTINAX!"

"NO, NO, IT'S NIGER!"

"I HEARD IT WAS CLODIUS ALBINUS..."

"WELL, NOBODY KNOWS!"

"NO, THAT WAS LAST MONTH. IT'S DIDIUS JULIANUS NOW!"

"ANYONE UP FOR SOME FOOD?"

The chaos ended when Septimius Severus took his army and marched on Rome. Severus took charge, putting his own guards in place, and sorting out all the small rebellions that had sprung up during the civil wars. By AD 197, he was the master of the whole Roman world.

Some people think the start of the fall of the Roman Empire actually began with Severus. By raising the pay for the army, and then training even more soldiers so he could invade more lands, he was spending a lot of Rome's money. He also gave donations to the people, and made many changes. Some people think that all this happening in a short time led to **TURMOIL** in Rome, and a city that is always at war with itself can't keep an eye on its massive empire quite so well...

THE CRISIS OF THE THIRD CENTURY

- Gallic Empire
- Roman Empire
- Palmyrene Empire

IT'S TIME TO BREAK UP

It was **AD** 235 to **AD** 284. With all the chaos of the last few hundred years, things were starting to fall apart. The Empire split into three parts. A man named **P**ostumus created the **G**allic **E**mpire (shown in green on the map). In **AD** 270, a queen called Zenobia took over the **P**almyrene **E**mpire (shown in yellow on the map). What was left was controlled by Rome.

QUEEN ZENOBIA

EAST MEETS WEST

The Roman Empire was now divided in a way it would never recover from. Diocletian split the empire further into four parts. Each part was ruled by a different leader.

> SEE ALL THAT GREEN, RIGHT THERE? GO ON. POINT TO IT. IT'S ALL MINE! I'M IN CHARGE AROUND THESE PARTS AND THAT'S JUST FINE BY ME. CAN YOU IMAGINE TRYING TO THINK ABOUT THIS WHOLE MAP? IT WOULD BE ENOUGH TO DRIVE YOU CRAZY... YOU'D END UP MAKING YOUR HORSE A CONSUL OR SOMETHING! HOW RIDICULOUS!

Diocletian and Maximian's idea to split the empire into four was working well. Each emperor could look after a smaller area of **TERRITORY** and keep everything running smoothly. Diocletian was the overall emperor, and Maximian was second to him. They were both known as **Augustus**. Each then adopted a son who would rule the smaller parts of the empire. These adopted sons were known as **Caesars** and they would eventually become the new **Augustuses**.

Diocletian chose a commander, a man named Constantius. Maximian chose a soldier, Galerius. Each Caesar had to answer to his adopted father, the Augustus. When the time came for them to take over, they should have had a lot of practice being a ruler. Was this the idea that would save the Roman Empire?

> HEY, I'M CONSTANTIUS. I'VE BEEN RULING OVER HERE IN THE EAST FOR A WHILE NOW. I'VE CHOSEN MY SON AS MY HEIR. AND I'VE NAMED HIM AFTER ME! BEING A CAESAR IS GREAT!

WAIT, WHAT?
TO PRONOUNCE THESE WORDS, SAY:

CONSTANTIUS = CON-STAN-TEE-US

GALERIUS = GAL-AIR-EE-US

CAESAR = SEE-ZER

CONSTANTINE

ANOTHER NEW EMPIRE?

After the deaths of the four emperors, there was some disagreement over who should rule, and how. And by "some disagreement" we mean war and chaos. Again. But why? Well, after each Augustus died, the Caesars moved up and named their own Caesars. However, neither man named their own actual son as Caesar, and the sons weren't too happy about it. Constantius's son, Constantine, and Maximian's son, Maxentius, got themselves declared emperor by their own armies. Can you guess what happened next? I mean, we are talking about the Romans here. They don't settle disagreements over a nice cup of tea…

LET'S TALK ABOUT JESUS CHRIST

Constantine defeated every challenger for this throne and was made SOLE emperor in AD 324. But there was something different about this new emperor. He was a Christian. For many years, it had been illegal to be Christian in Rome, and now the emperor himself was one! Constantine built a new capital city, naming it Constantinople. He filled it with churches, and Christianity grew and grew, eventually becoming the main religion of the empire. The old pagan gods were slowly forgotten.

THERE IS BUT ONE EMPEROR - ME! THERE IS BUT ONE GOD, AND THAT IS MY GOD! NOW NAME EVERYTHING AFTER ME. THE ROMAN EMPIRE IS SAVED!

TEA!

THIS IS WHAT THE ROMAN EMPIRE LOOKED LIKE WHEN CONSTANTINE WAS IN CHARGE.

THE GOTHS

If we go forwards a few years (and a few emperors), we arrive in AD 378. Rome was now a Christian city, and the empire was divided in two – Emperor Valens ruling the east and Emperor Valentinian the west. The Romans were still trying to conquer more land while continuing to fight with each other all the time. But now they had bigger problems...

WE'RE THE GOTHS AND WE'VE BEEN LIVING UP HERE IN THE COLD NORTH. WE'RE REALLY, REALLY TOUGH. WE'VE NOTICED THAT YOU ROMANS DON'T SEEM AS TOUGH AS YOU USED TO BE... SO WE'VE BEEN HAVING BATTLES WITH YOU FOR A WHILE NOW. WE DON'T CARE IF YOU THINK WE'RE BARBARIANS... WE WANT YOUR EMPIRE! AAAAARGGHHHHH!!

The Goths were headed for Constantinople. Valens, ruler of the Eastern Empire, took his forces to meet them but the Romans were confused and not ready. The Goths came down from the mountains like thunder, destroying the army and killing Valens. It was the worst Roman defeat for hundreds of years.

THIS IS THE BEGINNING OF THE END! I KNOW IT!

But those Romans knew how to hang on. The defeat was massive, but the next emperor was able to clean up the mess and make peace with the Goths. For a while...

WAIT, WHAT?
TO PRONOUNCE THESE WORDS, SAY

VALENS = VAL-ENZ

VALENTINIAN = VAL-EN-TIN-EE-AN

THE END OF THE WEST

(SPOILER ALERT)

Valens's grandsons, Arcadius and Honorius, took control around AD 393. They split the empire into two clear halves. The Eastern Empire was ruled by Arcadius and the Western Empire by Honorius. Honorius had real problems. The Goths, now split into two tribes (the Visigoths and the Ostrogoths), were attacking again and looking to invade. In AD 406, a tribe known as the Vandals from the **GERMANIC** area had crossed into the empire at Gaul and were heading for Hispania.

HONORIUS

> GOTHS TO THE LEFT OF ME, VANDALS TO THE RIGHT... HERE I AM. STUCK IN THE MIDDLE WITH... WELL, NOT AS MANY SOLDIERS AS I'D LIKE, AND BARBARIANS EVERYWHERE. AND THEY KEEP WINNING! I'M LOSING PARTS OF THE EMPIRE. THAT MEANS I'M ALSO LOSING SOLDIERS, AND MONEY. AT LEAST NO ONE HAS INVADED ROME...

WAIT, WHAT? WHERE ARE THOSE PLACES?

GAUL = MODERN-DAY FRANCE

HISPANIA = MODERN-DAY SPAIN AND PORTUGAL

24

INVASION OF ROME

On August 24, **AD** 410, the Visigoth King, Alaric, stormed Rome. For three days his troops **LOOTED AND PILLAGED** the city. It was the first time in 800 years that the city had fallen to a foreign enemy. Although it had been many years since Rome had been the capital of the Roman Empire, many historians agree that this was the first point in the true end of the Roman Empire in the west.

KING ALARIC

OH NO! ODOACER!

THE ABSOLUTE, REAL, ACTUAL END...

Some say that the last Roman emperor was Romulus Augustulus. Others (mostly people from the eastern empire at the time) say that he was a **PUPPET EMPEROR.** Romulus Augustulus was still a child when he became western emperor and his father Orestes was ruling until he was old enough. But by then, the Roman Empire was on its knees after many years of barbarian invasions and fighting among themselves. Rome was theirs for the taking...

HELLO, AUGUSTULUS. I AM ODOACER. I'VE DEFEATED YOUR TROOPS, I'VE EXECUTED ORESTES, AND I'M THE KING NOW. BUT LOOK. YOU'RE JUST A KID. IF YOU LET ME BE EMPEROR AND GIVE ME THAT SHINY CROWN, YOU CAN GO AND LIVE IN CAMPANIA. JUST DON'T COME BACK!

And that was it. With no Rome, no emperor, no Caesar, and with the empire itself split and broken beyond all recognition, the ancient Romans were gone...

HEY! AREN'T I THE GOD OF LIGHTNING ANYMORE? DOES THAT MEAN I CAN PUT THESE LIGHTNING BOLTS DOWN?

WHAT REMAINS OF THE ANCIENTS?

Italy today is a modern place, with bustling cities and a thriving culture all its own. But if you travel to modern-day Rome, you can still visit Roman temples and see the famous **MOSAICS**. Italy might be quite different now, but its history is all around us in the present day. Let's take a look at what the Romans left behind...

THE COLOSSEUM, WHERE GLADIATORS ONCE FOUGHT TO THE DEATH, STILL STANDS IN ROME. TOURISTS LIKE TO VISIT IT.

NEWSPAPERS

NEWS
WORLD ECONOMY BUSINESS TECHNOLOGIES SPORT ENTERTAINMENT MUSIC

The first newspaper was invented by Julius Caesar around 59 BC. It was called the Acta Diurna. It was carved in stone and displayed in a public place, to share important information with the people. Thankfully today, tablets are a little lighter...

MASS ENTERTAINMENT

The Romans loved to get together and have a good time. Theater, gladiator fights, and sporting events were a huge part of Roman life, and we still have a lot of their plays to see today.

GOVERNMENTS

THE ROMAN STYLE OF GOVERNMENT HELPED CREATE MANY OF THE GOVERNMENTS YOU SEE TODAY.

THE ROMAN FORUM

PLUMBING

ROADS

There is a saying: "All roads lead to Rome!" The Romans made really great roads, building over 50,000 miles of them across the empire. Roman roads are known for being long-lasting and straight.

ROMAN AQUEDUCTS TOOK WATER INTO THE CITIES AND ROMAN SEWERS TOOK DIRTY WATER AND HUMAN SEWAGE AWAY. IN SOME PLACES, THE ROMAN SEWERS WERE SO GOOD THAT THEY LASTED WELL INTO THE 1800s!

GLOSSARY

ADOPTION
when someone is made part of the family by choice instead of being related to the family

ASSASSINATED
killed for reasons having to do with power or religion

CIVIL WAR
a war between different groups in the same country

CONQUER
to overcome or take control of something by force

CONSUL
someone who is hired to look after a city in a different country

CULTURE
the way of life and traditions of a group of people

DAUGHTERS-IN-LAW
daughters who are part of a family because of marriage, instead of being related to anyone

FAMINES
times when large numbers of people do not have enough food

GERMANIC
having to do with the area of Europe around Germany

HEIR
someone who will get the objects, money, and titles of a person who dies

ICONIC
when something is well known and a symbol of a place or time

LEGIONARIES
Roman soldiers

LOOTED AND PILLAGED
to have stolen from a place using force and violence

LYRE
an ancient musical instrument that was a bit like a guitar

MOSAICS
pictures or patterns that are created by putting together small pieces of stone, tile, or glass

POLITICIAN
a person involved with politics and how the country is run

PROVINCE
an area that belongs to a certain country or empire

PUPPET EMPEROR
an emperor who has no real power and is controlled by someone else

REIGN
the time that a certain leader rules for

SEWAGE
water and waste material from humans

SOLE
the only one

TERRITORY
an area of land claimed and controlled by a country or empire

TURMOIL
a state of confusion, uncertainty, or upset

INDEX

B
baths 7
Byzantine Empire 27

C
Christians 2, 21–22
Constantinople 21, 23

E
emperors
- Antonius Pius 13
- Arcadius 24
- Augustus 8–9, 18–20
- Aurelian 17
- Caligula 10–11, 14
- Commodus 14
- Constantine 20–21
- Constantius 19–20
- Diocletian 17–19
- Domitian 11–12
- Galerius 19
- Hadrian 13
- Honorius 24
- Marcus Aurelius 8-9, 13–14
- Maxentius 20
- Maximian 17–20
- Nero 11, 14
- Nerva 12
- Romulus Augustulus 26
- Septimius Severus 15
- Trajan 12–13
- Valens 22–24
- Valentinian 22–23

G
Gaul 24
generals 6, 12
gladiators 4, 6, 27–29
gods 4, 7, 10, 21, 26
- Jupiter 4, 7
- Mars 4
Goths 22–25
- Ostrogoths 24
- Visigoths 24–25

H
Hispania 24

L
legionaries 4, 6

M
materfamilias 7

O
Odoacer 26

P
Pagans 21
paterfamilias 7
Pax Romana 8–9
Postumus 16–17

Q
Queen Zenobia 16

S
slave 7

PHOTO CREDITS

All images are courtesy of Shutterstock.com, unless otherwise specified. With thanks to Getty Images, Thinkstock Photo and iStockphoto. Front Cover – Phant, ZaZa Studio, Andrey Yurlov, Merfin, spaxiax, AikStudio. 4&5 – Karl Allen Lugmayer, Razvan Stroie, Africa Studio, polkadot_photo, Hunter Bliss Images, Denis Zyatkov. 6&7 – Wilson Marcius, Natursports, Vuk Kostic, Luis Louro, delcarmat, Diego Delso. 8&9 – FooTToo, pcruciatti, Morphart Creation. 10&11 – PLRANG ART, Gilmanshin, Jackknife Barlow. 12&13 – Framo, Anagoria, riekephotos, Sara Winter, Yulliii. 14&15 – MZeta, José Luiz Bernardes Ribeiro, José Luiz Bernardes Ribeiro. 16&17 – Janusz Pienkowski, Creative Commons: Attribution-ShareAlike, Jebulon. 18&19 – Coppermine Photo Gallery, Rasiel Suarez, ashva. 20&21 – Regien Paassen, Natalia Paklina, Karl Spruner von Merz [Public domain]. 22&23 – Kachalkina Veronika, Meilun. 24&25 – lynea, Augustine, La Cité de Dieu (Vol. I). Translation from the Latin by Raoul de Presles, Ludwig Thiersch [Public domain]. 28&29 – Leszek Bogdewicz, Meiqianbao, d13, Fotokvadrat, Kiev.Victor, steve estvanik. Paper – ZaZa Studio, Monica Butnaru, Ints Vikmanis, ZaZa Studio, Anton Watman. Speech Bubbles – Nataleana. Caption banner – Olga_C